T0035792

by Laurie Calkhoven
illustrated by Monique Dong

Ready-to-Read

Simon Spotlight
New York London Toronto Sydney New Delhi

SIMON SPOTLIGHT
An imprint of Simon & Schuster Children's Publishing Division
1230 Avenue of the Americas, New York, New York 10020
This Simon Spotlight edition May 2023

Manufactured in the United States of America 0323 LAK
2 4 6 8 10 9 7 5 3 1
This book has been cataloged with the Library of Congress.
ISBN 978-1-6659-3342-1 (hc)
ISBN 978-1-6659-3341-4 (pbk)
ISBN 978-1-6659-3343-8 (ebook)

CONTENTS

Introduction

Do you love to run and to play games with your friends? Do you wonder what it would be like to show off your skills and win those games in front of the whole world?

You should meet the women of the US women's national soccer team! Team USA has won more Women's World Cup championships than any other soccer team in history.

These players all got started kicking the ball in parks and schoolyards. They played on boys' teams when there weren't teams for girls. They wore hand-me-down uniforms, and they never gave up. They showed the world that anything is possible if only you dare to dream.

These players are unstoppable!

Chapter 1
A History of US Women's Soccer

Women and girls have been playing soccer for a long time. The first recorded women's match took place in Scotland in 1881. Women's soccer clubs popped up in England and in other parts of Europe. But in the 1900s, many people (mostly men) thought soccer was too hard for women and girls. They said running and kicking would be bad for girls. They thought girls would hurt themselves if they ran too much and kicked too hard.

Did girls agree? No—they wanted to play! Girls kicked soccer balls around with friends or played with their brothers. But there were no teams for them to join.

In the 1970s women's soccer teams were created in Europe, Asia, and South America. The United States was behind the rest of the world. Soccer wasn't popular in the US for men or women.

But things were starting to change.

In 1972 the US passed a law called Title IX (Title Nine). The law said that schools had to treat boys and girls equally. If schools had sports for boys, they had to have sports for girls, too.

Girls across the country were ready to play. Towns, high schools, and colleges formed soccer teams.

It wasn't long before women's soccer became one of the most popular sports in the US. It was even more popular than men's soccer! The most popular team was from the University of North Carolina (UNC).

In 1985, the US formed the first women's national team (USWNT). Team USA had almost no money to travel to games. They had to sew hand-me-down men's uniforms to fit. They were not the team to beat. Out of the four teams competing in their first international tournament in 1985, they came in fourth place.

FIFA
WOMEN'S
WORLD CUP

The coach from UNC, Anson Dorrance, took over the national team. He looked all over the country for the best players. Team USA began to win games and even made it to the finals in tournaments.

By the time of the first Women's World Cup in 1991, Team USA was ready to take on the best teams in the world. They were ready to be champions.

Today, they are the most successful women's soccer team in the world!

Chapter 2
The World Cup

The International Federation of Association Football, known as FIFA, oversees soccer around the world. Since 1930, there has been a World Cup match for men's teams every four years (except in 1942 and 1946, when it was not held because of World War II). Countries from all over the world take part. And sports fans from all over the world tune in!

In 1991, FIFA added a Women's World Cup contest. This contest also takes place every four years. And can you guess which team has won more World Cup finals than any other? Team USA!

Chapter 3
1991 Women's World Cup

The first Women's World Cup match was played in China. FIFA didn't expect a lot of people to buy tickets. But almost sixty-five thousand fans were in the stands for the final game.

Team USA wowed the world. They won every game to reach the finals. The final match against Norway was their toughest. But they beat Norway 2–1 (two goals to one). Now the world knew that Team USA was the team to watch.

There was just one problem. The games weren't widely aired. The women on the team were still wearing hand-me-down uniforms. They had hardly any money for travel or training.

If American women's soccer was going to be successful, they needed the American people to pay attention.

Chapter 4

1999 Women's World Cup

At the 1995 World Cup, Team USA came in third.

In 1999 the games were being held in the United States for the first time. Team USA wanted to be first again. They also had to fill big stadiums with fans. The players from Team USA visited girls' soccer clubs across the country to talk about the World Cup. Girls got excited and bought tickets to the games. The US won the first game in front of almost

eighty thousand fans in Giants Stadium, one of the biggest football stadiums in the country. They won every game to reach the final match against the team from China. The games were now nationally aired, and millions watched the two best teams compete on TV.

At the end of the game, the score was 0–0. The teams took turns, each making five shots at the goal, to find a winner. The first four players were successful. The score was 2–2. Then Briana Scurry, the goalkeeper, blocked one kicker from Team China. The next two players scored. The score was 4–4 when Brandi Chastain from Team USA stepped up to take the very last kick.

Whoosh! The ball blew past the goalkeeper from Team China. Team USA won the World Cup! This time, girls all over America were watching. Soccer became the game girls wanted to play!

WOMEN'S WORLD CUP
15
9

Chapter 5
2015 Women's World Cup

Team USA made it to the top three in the next three Women's World Cups in 2003, 2007, and 2011, but they did not win. Top three is great, but they wanted to be world champions again.

In the 2015 games in Canada, Team USA knocked out team after team to reach the final match. This time, they faced Team Japan—the team that had knocked them out of the 2011 competition.

The US took a 4–0 lead in just sixteen minutes. Carli Lloyd made the fastest hat trick (three goals in one game) in women's soccer history. Lauren Holiday made a fourth goal.

Japan didn't give up. But in the end the score was 5–2. Team USA became the first team ever to win three Women's World Cup titles!

Chapter 6
2019 Women's World Cup

Team USA entered the World Cup in France ready to defend their title. They defeated six teams to reach the final. The Netherlands made the final for the very first time. They wanted to bring a victory home. Team USA was ready to fight for the title.

For the first hour of the game, neither team was able to score a goal. Then US team captain Megan Rapinoe made a penalty kick.

Goal!

Eight minutes later Team USA scored a second goal. The game ended with a 2–1 victory for the US, giving Team USA their fourth World Cup win!

Chapter 7
Soccer Stars!

Megan Rapinoe

Megan Rapinoe was born on July 5, 1985, in Redding, California. She is the youngest of six children. Her twin sister, Rachael, is eleven minutes older. Megan started playing soccer when she was four. Today, soccer fans all over the world know her for her famous pose—arms out wide and chin up—and her pink, purple, and green hair.

There were no girls' soccer teams where she lived, so Megan and her sister played on boys' teams. In high school she was on the track team and the basketball team and played soccer.

In college, Megan focused on soccer, and the world noticed. In 2011 and 2015, playing forward, she helped Team USA come in second and first at the World Cup. Megan was co-captain when Team USA headed to the 2019 World Cup. In the final against the Netherlands, she was the first to score. She won every award a soccer player can win in those games!

Megan is also busy off the field. She spoke out for equal pay for women. She came out as gay in 2012. And she always stands up for what she thinks is right.

Go, Megan!

Briana Scurry

Goalkeeper Briana Scurry, who was born on September 7, 1971, always had energy for sports! She got her start playing football on boys' teams in the suburbs of Minneapolis, Minnesota. In middle school, she tried out for soccer and was made goalkeeper on the boys' team. She was also a basketball and track-and-field star. In college, she concentrated on soccer.

There were just a few African American women in soccer at the time. Briana opened doors for other Black players.

Briana blocked a penalty kick in the final match of the 1999 World Cup. That made it possible for Team USA to win. Suddenly, Americans were paying attention to soccer. And now the whole world knew Briana was a star!

She went on to play in the first women's pro soccer league and was one of the first players to come out as gay. A head injury ended her career as a player. She went on to become a coach, wrote a book about her life, and reviews soccer matches on TV. She's a real champion!

13

Alex Morgan

Forward Alex Morgan played her first World Cup game for Team USA in 2011. Born on July 2, 1989, in San Dimas, California, Alex played lots of different sports growing up. Her dad was her soccer coach.

Alex played soccer in college and joined the US women's national team in 2010. In the final minutes of a game that would decide if Team USA would play in the 2011 World Cup, she scored the winning goal! She was the youngest player on the World Cup team and managed to score goals against the teams from France and Japan. In 2015 she helped Team USA go all the way to win the World Cup.

Equal pay for women is important to Alex. She joined Megan Rapinoe and other players to speak up for women's rights.

Today she's still one of the greatest players in the world and takes the time to inspire girls. She wrote a series of books called The Kicks and even has a Barbie Shero doll that looks just like her. "Keep striving for your goals, because one day you can be living that dream you once had as a child," she said.

Alex Morgan is living her dream!

GO FOR YOUR GOALS!"
13
ALEX MORGAN
13
13
13
MORGAN
ALEX MORGAN
ALEX MORGAN

Trinity Rodman

Forward Trinity Rodman was just four years old when she started playing soccer. The daughter of basketball great Dennis Rodman, Trinity tried lots of sports. She decided that soccer was the game for her.

Trinity was born on May 20, 2002, and grew up in Laguna Niguel, California. She was a soccer star all through school. In 2021 she joined a professional team, the Washington Spirits. Just minutes into her first game, the eighteen-year-old became the youngest player to score a goal in National Women's Soccer League history.

Trinity went on to be named 2021 Rookie of the Year. As of 2022, she's also the highest-paid player in the National Women's Soccer League.

But Trinity didn't stop there. She joined Team USA when she was nineteen. She played in her first game against the Czech Republic and scored her first goal for the team in her second game!

As of May 2023, Trinity hasn't played in a World Cup match yet. Will she help Team USA win the Cup in July 2023? It's too soon to say. But keep your eye on her. She can't be stopped!

9

Mia Hamm

Mariel Margaret "Mia" Hamm was the US's first female soccer star. She was born on March 17, 1972, in Selma, Alabama. Her father was in the air force, and the family moved a lot. Soccer helped Mia make new friends in new schools.

Mia was born with a clubfoot, which means that one foot was twisted. She wore casts on her feet to fix the problem. As soon as they came off, she started running! She joined her first soccer team when she was five. By middle school, she was playing on the boys' team.

When she was fifteen, Mia became the youngest person ever on the US women's national team. She played forward for the next seventeen years, helping Team USA win two World Cups and two Olympic gold medals.

When she retired in 2004, she had scored the most goals—158—of any male or female player in international competition. Her record held until Abby Wambach broke it in 2013.

Mia is often described as the best women's soccer player in history. She put soccer on the map and opened doors for thousands of young players.

Mia never stopped going for the goal!

BUT WAIT . . .

THERE'S MORE!

Turn the page to learn some soccer skills, read a short history of soccer, and find some fun soccer trivia facts.

Learn Three Beginner Soccer Skills

Dribbling

Just like in basketball, dribbling is the most important skill to know in soccer. To start, you need to keep your knees bent just a little and lean forward a bit. This position will keep you ready to quickly move in other directions. You should also keep your arms loose and let them move around as much as they want to. They are an important part of keeping your balance! When it comes to moving the ball, it's better to kick the soccer ball softly and frequently. You can use every part of your foot and be sure to keep the ball under your control! If you kick the ball too hard and too far, someone can take it from you. Be sure to keep the soccer ball close to you while you tap it across the field!

Juggling

Soccer players juggle too, but this kind of juggling is a little different from how you might have seen a clown juggle. To juggle like a soccer player, you have to use your feet instead of your hands. Remember, no hands in soccer! There are two important tips to learning this

trick. One, practice balancing on one foot. And two, be sure to keep your eye on the soccer ball to maintain your focus. Now let's start. First, put the ball on top of your dominant foot. Now that you have practiced your balance, softly kick the ball into the air with your dominant foot without letting the ball touch the ground. Keep practicing with one foot before moving on to the next.

The Drag Back

This trick can be done while you're standing or while you're dribbling and is a great way to change directions. To start, you're going to put your nondominant foot to the side of the soccer ball and your dominant foot on top of the ball. Your dominant foot is your stronger foot, and your nondominant foot is your weaker one. Remember, focus on your balance. You want to be sure your dominant foot is in the center of the soccer ball. If it's too far to one side, your foot might slip off the ball! Now that you have your dominant foot balanced on the center of the soccer ball, you're going to drag your foot backward on the ball and begin to dribble with your dominant foot, or with your other foot if you want to!

The History of Soccer

Dating as far back as 5000–300 BC and all the way up to the nineteenth century, many countries have been recorded playing some kind of game that resembles the soccer we all love today. Countries like China, Greece, Italy, Canada, the US, and parts of Central America have been a part of soccer's long history. But it was actually England that was responsible for building the foundation and rules for the game back in the 1800s.

Did You Know?

Soccer was originally only called football! Most places in the world still call it football, while very few call it soccer.

It wasn't until the 1860s that the Football Association was founded, and eleven London schools and clubs gathered at a meeting place and all agreed on one set of rules that they all had to follow if they ever played a game with each other.

Did You Know?

It wasn't always against the rules to touch the ball with your hands. It wasn't until 1869 that the Football Association made it a rule for all players to follow!

The first-ever official soccer match played (with rules) was in London on December 19, 1863, between Barnes Football Club and Richmond Football Club. That game ended with a 0–0 draw. The first international soccer match was played between Scotland and England on November 30, 1872. Then the International Football Association Board was formed in 1886. Soon after, the first international soccer match outside of Europe was played between the US and Canada, with Canada winning 1–0.

Soccer by the Numbers

More than fifteen hundred US colleges have women's soccer teams and more than fourteen hundred US colleges have men's soccer teams. All of those teams fall into one of five divisions: Division One, Division Two, Division Three, NAIA, and NJCAA.

There are 333 NCAA Division One women's soccer colleges and 205 NCAA Division One men's soccer colleges in the US.

Most well-known soccer leagues in the world play between thirty-four and thirty-eight games in one year.

Professional women's and men's soccer games are split into two 45-minute halves, which makes an entire soccer match ninety minutes long.

Between the two halves, both teams take a halftime break, which lasts fifteen minutes.

The world record for the longest soccer game is a game played in England for a charity called Kicking Off Against Cancer. The match lasted 169 hours!

The average soccer player runs seven to ten miles a game! But your average goalkeeper might run only two miles a game.

Now that you've met the women of the US women's national soccer team, what have you learned?

1. In the 1900s, why were women and girls told they couldn't play soccer?
a. They would not like it   b. They would get hurt   c. Male players were better

2. What obstacles did the USWNT face when they first started?
a. They had no supporters   b. They had no money to travel   c. Both a and b

3. Who was named 2021 Women's Soccer Rookie of the Year?
a. Mia Hamm   b. Trinity Rodman   c. Megan Rapinoe

4. Which of these statements is true?
a. The men's World Cup takes place every two years and the women's World Cup takes place every four years   b. The men's World Cup started in 1991
c. The men's World Cup started in 1930

5. Which professional women's soccer player played on a boys' soccer team first?
a. Megan Rapinoe   b. Mia Hamm   c. Both a and b

6. Who played her first World Cup game for Team USA in 2011?
a. Alex Morgan   b. Trinity Rodman   c. Mia Hamm

7. How long did it take Team USA to score in the final game of the 2019 Women's World Cup?
a. 8 minutes   b. 23 minutes   c. Over 60 minutes

8. What do Alex Morgan and Trinity Rodman have in common?
a. They both have fathers involved in sports   b. They were both named Rookie of the Year   c. They both scored goals to win a World Cup

9. What law says if schools have sports for boys, they have to have sports for girls too?
a. Title XI   b. Title IV   c. Title IX

10. When did FIFA add a Women's World Cup every four years?
a. 1991   b. 2001   c. 1981

Answers: 1.b 2.c 3.b 4.c 5.c 6.a 7.c 8.a 9.c 10.a